MW00615644

LEAVES OF
COMFORT AND
INSPIRATION

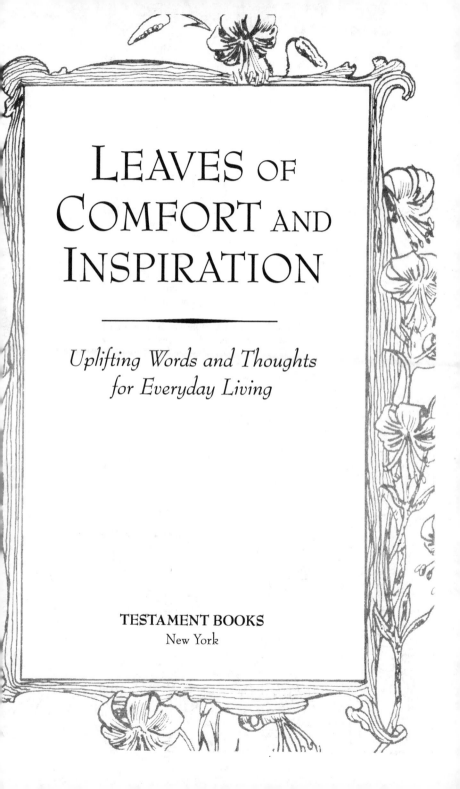

LEAVES OF COMFORT AND INSPIRATION

*Uplifting Words and Thoughts
for Everyday Living*

TESTAMENT BOOKS
New York

This 2000 edition is published by Testament Books™,
an imprint of Random House Value Publishing, Inc.,
280 Park Avenue, New York, New York 10017.

This book was originally published as two separate volumes:
Leaves of Comfort and *Leaves of Inspiration*.

Testament Books™ and design are trademarks of
Random House Value Publishing, Inc.

Random House
New York • Toronto • London • Sydney • Auckland
http://www.randomhouse.com/

Printed and bound in the United States of America

A CIP catalog record for this book is available
from the Library of Congress.

ISBN 0-517-16222-9

8 7 6 5 4 3 2 1

LEAVES OF COMFORT

FOREWORD

"The lowest ebb is the turn of the tide."
Henry Wadsworth Longfellow

Leaves of Comfort is a collection of quotations for the difficult times in our lives—times of loss, serious illness, pain or grief. At these moments we feel alone and vulnerable, in need of comfort and support.

Leaves of Comfort offers the wisdom of well-known writers—Robert Louis Stevenson, Mark Twain, Henry Wadsworth Longfellow, Victor Hugo, George Eliot, William Shakespeare, Rudyard Kipling and others—to strengthen us and give us a feeling of universal fellowship.

Although the words in *Leaves of Comfort* cannot erase all our pain and grief, we can find solace and a lessening of sorrow by sharing the thoughts and feelings of others who have been in similar situations.

Pain and loss are part of the human experience, but they do not have to destroy us. They can help us to a fuller appreciation of life, to the realization that our darkest moments will pass and that what we thought was our lowest ebb actually is the turn of the tide.

ELEGY WRITTEN IN A COUNTRY CHURCHYARD

The curfew tolls the knell of parting day,
  The lowing herds wind slowly o'er the lea,
The ploughman homeward plods his weary way,
  And leaves the world to darkness and to me.

Now fades the glimmering landscape on the sight,
  And all the air a solemn stillness holds,
Save where the beetle wheels his droning flight,
  And drowsy tinklings lull the distant folds:

Save that from yonder ivy-mantled tower,
  The moping owl does to the moon complain
Of such as, wand'ring near her secret bower,
  Molest her ancient, solitary reign.

Beneath those rugged elms, that yew-trees' shade,
  Where heaves the turf in many a mold'ring heap,
Each in his narrow cell forever laid,
  The rude forefathers of the hamlet sleep.

The breezy call of incense-breathing morn,
  The swallow twitt'ring from the straw-built shed,
The cock's shrill clarion, of the echoing morn,
  No more shall rouse them from their lowly bed.

For them no more the blazing hearth shall burn,
  Or busy housewife ply her evening care;
No children run to lisp their sire's return,
  Or climb his knees the envied kiss to share.

Oft did the harvest to their sickle yield,
    Their furrow oft the stubborn glebe has broke;
How jocund did they drive their team afield!
    How bowed the woods beneath their sturdy stroke!

Let not ambition mock their useful toil,
    Their homely joys, and destiny obscure;
Nor grandeur hear with a disdainful smile
    The short and simple annals of the poor.

The boast of heraldry, the pomp of pow'r,
    And all that beauty, all that wealth e'er gave,
Await alike th' inevitable hour.
    The paths of glory head but to the grave.

Nor you, ye proud, impute to these the fault,
    If memory o'er their tomb no trophies raise,
Where thro' the long-drawn aisle and fretted vault,
    The pealing anthem swells the note of praise.

Can storied urn, or animated bust,
Back to its mansion call the fleeting breath?
Can honor's voice provoke the silent dust,
    Or flatt'ry soothe the dull cold ear of Death?

Perhaps in this neglected spot is laid
    Some heart once pregnant with celestial fire;
Hands that the rod of empire might have sway'd,
    Or waked to ecstasy the living lyre.

But knowledge to their eyes her ample page,
  Rich with the spoils of time, did ne'er unroll;
Chill penury repressed their noble rage,
  And froze the genial current of the soul.

Full many a gem of purest ray serene
  The dark unfathomed caves of ocean bear;
Full many a flower is born to blush unseen,
  And waste its sweetness on the desert air.

Thomas Gray

IF WE HAD THE TIME

If I had the time to find a place
And sit me down full face to face
With my better self that stands no show
In my daily life that rushes so,
It might be then I would see my soul
Was stumbling still toward the shining goal—
I might be nerved by the thought sublime,
    If I had the time!

If I had the time to let my heart
Speak out and take in my life a part,
To look about and stretch a hand
To a comrade quartered on no-luck land,
Ah, God! If I might but just sit still
And hear the note of the whip-poor-will,
I think that my wish with God would rhyme—
    If I had the time!

If I had the time to learn from you
How much for comfort my word would do;
And I told you then of my sudden will
To kiss your feet when I did you ill—
If the tears aback of the bravado
Could force their way and let you know—
Brothers, the souls of us all would chime,
    If we had the time!

THE LORD IS MY SHEPHERD!

1 The Lord is my shepherd; I shall not want.

2 He maketh me to lie down in green pastures; he leadeth me beside the still waters.

3 He restoreth my soul; he leadeth me in the paths of righteousness for his name's sake.

4 Yea, though I walk through the valley of the shadow of death, I will fear no evil; for thou art with me; thy rod and they staff they comfort me.

5 Thou preparest a table before me in the presence of mine enemies; thou anointest my head with oil; my cup runneth over.

6 Surely goodness and mercy shall follow me all the days of my life; and I will dwell in the house of the Lord forever.

Psalms XXIII

NOW I LAY ME DOWN TO SLEEP

Now I lay me down to sleep,
I pray Thee, Lord, my soul to keep.
If I should die before I wake
I pray Thee, Lord, my soul to take
And this I ask for Jesus' sake.
Amen.

HORACE GREELEY'S SORROW

My Friend:—The loss of my boy makes a great change in my feelings, plans and prospects. The joy of my life was comprehended in his, and I do not now feel that any personal object can strongly move me henceforth. I had thought of buying a country place, but it was for him. I had begun to love flowers and beautiful objects, because he liked them. Now, all that deeply concerns me is the evidence that we shall live hereafter, and especially that we shall live with and know those we loved here. I mean to act my part while life is spared me, but I no longer covet length of days. If I felt sure on the point of identifying and being with our loved ones in the world to come, I would prefer not to live long. As it is, I am resigned to whatever may be divinely ordered. . . . We had but few hours to prepare for our loss. He went to bed as hearty and happy as ever. At 5 A. M. he died. . . . His mother had bought him a fiddle the day before, which delighted him beyond measure; and he was only induced to lay it up at night by his delight at the idea of coming up in the morning and surprising me by playing on it before I got up. In the morning at daylight I was called to his bedside. The next day, I followed him to his grave! You cannot guess how golden and lovely his long hair (never cut) looked in the coffin. . . . Pickie was five years old last March. So much grace and wit and poetry were rarely or never blended in so young a child,

14

and to us his form and features were the perfection of beauty. We can never have another child, and life cannot be long enough to efface, though it will temper this sorrow. It differs in kind as well as degree from all that we have hitherto experienced.

15

GOD MOVES IN A MYSTERIOUS WAY

God moves in a mysterious way
  His wonders to perform;
He plants his footsteps in the sea,
  And rides upon the storm.

Deep in unfathomable mines,
  With never-failing skill,
He treasures up his bright designs,
  And works his sovereign will.

Judge not the Lord by feeble sense,
  But trust him for his grace;
Behind a frowning providence
  He hides a smiling face.

His purposes will ripen fast,
  Unfolding every hour;
The bud may have a bitter taste,
  But sweet will be the flower.

Blind unbelief is sure to err,
  And scan his work in vain;
God is his own interpreter,
  And he will make it plain.

16

Ye fearful saints fresh courage take,
  The clouds you so much dread
Are big with mercy and shall break,
  With blessings on your head.

                    William Cowper

A JUNE MORNING

Oh! have you not seen on some morning in June,
When the flowers were in tears and the forest in
   tune,
When the billows of morn broke bright on the air,
On the breast of the brightest, some star clinging
   there?
Some sentinel star not ready to set,
Forgetting to wane and watching there yet?

How you gazed on that vision of beauty the while,
How it wavered till torn by the light of God's smile,
How it passed through the portals of pearl like a
   bride,
How it paled as it passed and the morning star
   died.
The sky was all blushes; the lark was all bliss,
And the prayer of your heart was "Be my ending
   like this."

So my beautiful dove passed away from life's even;
So the blush of her being was blended with heaven;
So the bird of my bosom fluttered up in the dawn,
A window was open; my darling was gone.
A truant from tears, from time and from sin,
For the angel on watch took the wanderer in.

And when I shall hear the new song that she sings
I shall know her again, notwithstanding her wings,
By those eyes full of heaven; by the light of her
    hair,
And the smile she wore here she will surely wear
    there.

THE DAY IS DONE

The day is done, and the darkness
   Falls from the wings of Night,
As a feather is wafted downward
   From an eagle in his flight.

I see the lights of the village
   Gleam through the rain and the mist,
And a feeling of sadness comes o'er me
   That my soul cannot resist:

A feeling of sadness and longing,
   That is not akin to pain,
And resembles sorrow only
   As the mist resembles the rain.

Come, read to me some poem,
   Some simple and heartfelt lay,
That shall soothe this restless feeling,
   And banish the thoughts of day.

Not from the grand old masters,
   Not from the bards sublime,
Whose distant footsteps echo
   Through the corridors of Time.

For like strains of martial music,
   Their mighty thoughts suggest
Life's endless toil and endeavor;
   And tonight I long for rest.

20

Read from some humbler poet,
　　Whose songs gushed from his heart,
As showers from the clouds of summer,
　　Or tears from the eyelids start;

Who, through long days of labor,
　　And nights devoid of ease,
Still heard in his soul the music
　　Of wonderful melodies.

Such songs have power to quiet
　　The restless pulse of care,
And come like the benediction
　　That follows after prayer.

Then read from the treasured volume
　　The poem of thy choice,
And lend to the rhyme of the poet
　　The beauty of thy voice.

And the night shall be filled with music,
　　And the cares that infest the day,
Shall fold their tents like the Arabs,
　　And as silently steal away.

Henry W. Longfellow

21

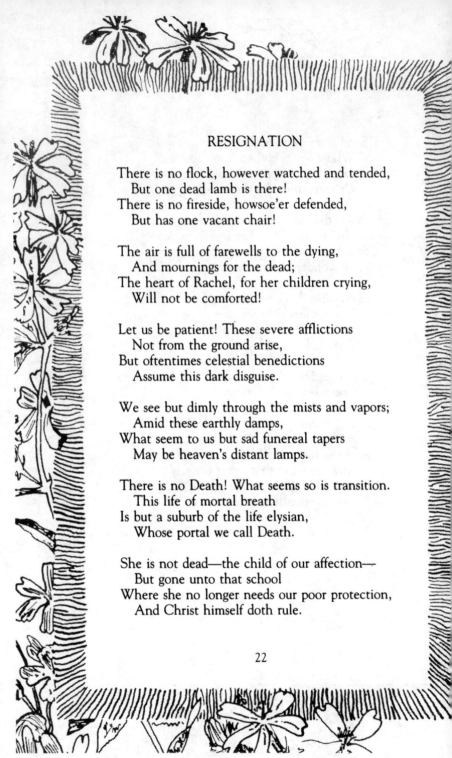

RESIGNATION

There is no flock, however watched and tended,
    But one dead lamb is there!
There is no fireside, howsoe'er defended,
    But has one vacant chair!

The air is full of farewells to the dying,
    And mournings for the dead;
The heart of Rachel, for her children crying,
    Will not be comforted!

Let us be patient! These severe afflictions
    Not from the ground arise,
But oftentimes celestial benedictions
    Assume this dark disguise.

We see but dimly through the mists and vapors;
    Amid these earthly damps,
What seem to us but sad funereal tapers
    May be heaven's distant lamps.

There is no Death! What seems so is transition.
    This life of mortal breath
Is but a suburb of the life elysian,
    Whose portal we call Death.

She is not dead—the child of our affection—
    But gone unto that school
Where she no longer needs our poor protection,
    And Christ himself doth rule.

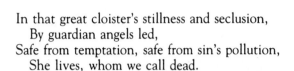

In that great cloister's stillness and seclusion,
   By guardian angels led,
Safe from temptation, safe from sin's pollution,
   She lives, whom we call dead.

Day after day we think what she is doing
   In those bright realms of air;
Year after year, her tender steps pursuing,
   Behold her grown more fair.

Thus do we walk with her, and keep unbroken
   The bond which nature gives,
Thinking that our remembrance, though unspoken,
   May reach her where she lives.

Not as a child shall we again behold her
   For when with raptures wild
In our embraces we again enfold her,
   She will not be a child;

But a fair maiden, in her Father's mansion,
   Clothed with celestial grace;
And beautiful with all the soul's expansion
   Shall we behold her face.

And though at times impetuous with emotion
   And anguish long suppressed,
The swelling heart heaves moaning like the ocean,
   That cannot be at rest.

23

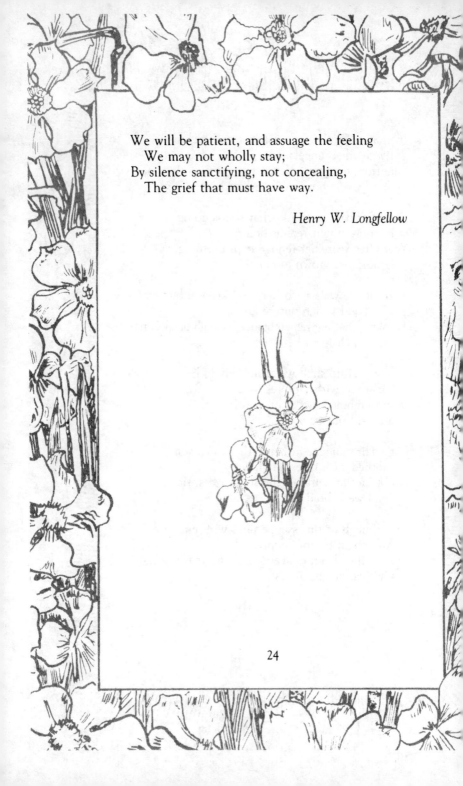

We will be patient, and assuage the feeling
  We may not wholly stay;
By silence sanctifying, not concealing,
  The grief that must have way.

Henry W. Longfellow

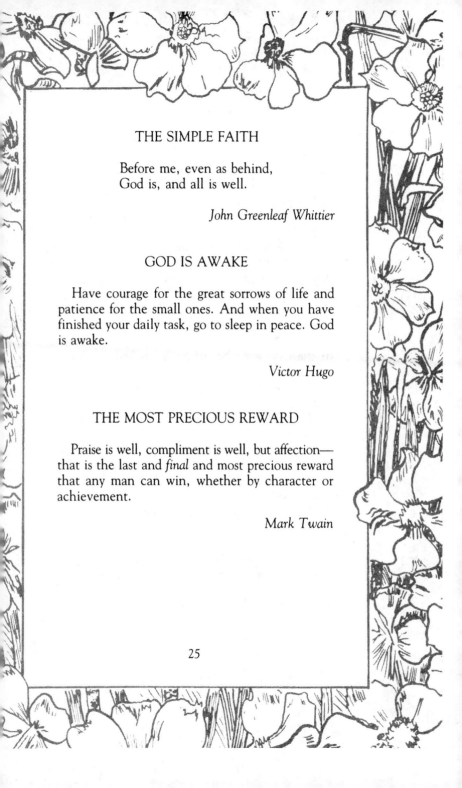

THE SIMPLE FAITH

Before me, even as behind,
God is, and all is well.

John Greenleaf Whittier

GOD IS AWAKE

Have courage for the great sorrows of life and patience for the small ones. And when you have finished your daily task, go to sleep in peace. God is awake.

Victor Hugo

THE MOST PRECIOUS REWARD

Praise is well, compliment is well, but affection—that is the last and *final* and most precious reward that any man can win, whether by character or achievement.

Mark Twain

25

THE DAYS GONE BY

Oh, the days gone by! Oh, the days gone by!
The apples in the orchard, and the pathway through
the rye;
The chirrup of the robin, and the whistle of the
quail
As he piped across the meadows sweet as any
night ingale;
When the bloom was on the clover and the blue
was in the sky,
And my happy heart brimmed over in the days
gone by.

In the days gone by, when my naked feet were
tripped
By the honeysuckle tangles where the water lilies
dripped,
And the ripples of the river lipped the moss along
the brink
Where the placid-eyed and lazy-footed cattle came
to drink,
And the tilting snipe stood fearless of the truant's
wayward cry
And the splashing of the swimmer, in the days
gone by.

Oh, the days gone by! Oh, the days gone by!
The music of the laughing lip, the luster of the
eye;
The childish faith in fairies, and Aladdin's magic
ring—

The simple, soul-reposing glad belief in everything—
When life was like a story, holding neither sob nor
   sigh,
In the golden olden glory of the days gone by.

James Whitcomb Riley

27

ROCK OF AGES—THE HYMN

Rock of Ages, cleft for me,
Let me hide myself in Thee.
Let the water and the blood
From thy riven side which flowed,
Be of sin the double cure.
Save from guilt and make me pure.

Could my tears forever flow;
Could my seal no languor know;
These for sin could not atone,
Thou must save, and Thou alone.
Rock of Ages cleft for me,
Let me hide myself in thee.

Not the labor of my hands
Can fulfill Thy law's demands;
Could my seal no respite know,
Could my tears forever flow,
All for sin could not atone;
Thou must save and Thou alone.

Nothing in my hand I bring;
Simply to Thy cross I cling.
Naked, come to Thee for dress,
Helpless, look to Thee for grace.
Foul, I to the Fountain fly,
Wash me, Savior, or I die.

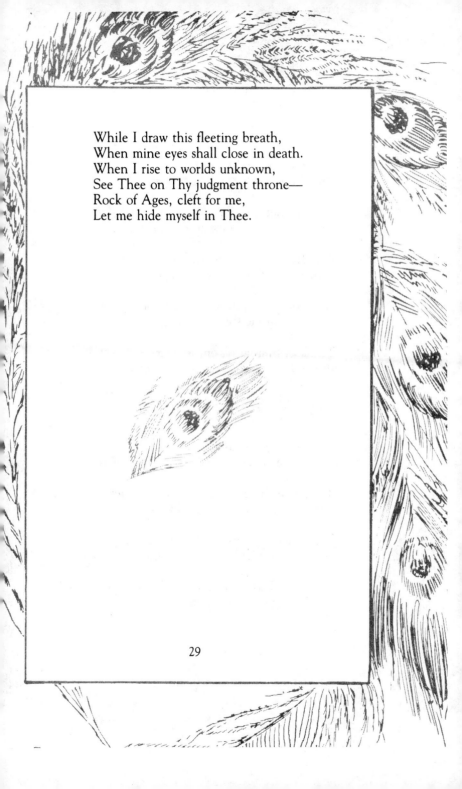

While I draw this fleeting breath,
When mine eyes shall close in death,
When I rise to worlds unknown,
See Thee on Thy judgment throne—
Rock of Ages, cleft for me,
Let me hide myself in Thee.

AWAY

I cannot say, and I will not say
That he is dead. He is just away!

With a cheery smile and a wave of the hand,
He has wandered into an unknown land,

And left us dreaming how very fair
It needs must be, since he lingers there.

And you—oh, you, who the wildest yearn
for the old-time step and the glad return—

Think of him faring on, as dear
In the love of There as the love of Here;

And loyal still, as he gave the blows
Of his warrior stength to his country's foes—

Mild and gentle, as he was brave,
When the sweetest love of his life he gave

To simple things; where the violets grew
Pure as the eyes they were likened to,

The touches of his hands have strayed
As reverently as his lips have prayed;

When the little brown thrush that harshly chirred
Was dear to him as the mocking-bird;

And he pitied as much as a man in pain
A writhing honey-bee wet with rain.

Think of him still as the same, I say;
He is not dead—he is just—away!

James Whitcomb Riley

31

FOUND BY THE SHEPHERD

The sun from on high his glory flinging
    Filled all the land with a golden glow;
And the glad light fell o'er a mother singing
    A tender lullaby, sweet and low:
"My lamb! my lamb! may the Shepherd behold
    thee
    As He did the little ones of yore,
And safe in His loving arms enfold thee
    For evermore! Oh, for evermore!"

Ah me! ah me! o'er the brightest morning
    The storm may break and the storm-clouds fly;
And the fairest flowers life's path adorning
    Spring up and blossom but to die.
The sunlight fades and the shadows thicken,
    A chill wind blows from a far-off shore,
And the mother's arms, to her heart sore stricken,
    Shall clasp her darling—ah! nevermore.

But as the bright arch through the storm comes
    shining
    And tells of the mercy that cannot cease,
So now, through the storm of her sad repining,
    There comes a glad whisper of hope and peace:
"Thy lamb that was lost, lo! the Shepherd found it
    And safe to His own green pastures bore;
And the everlasting arms are around it
    For evermore! Oh, for evermore!"

I SHALL NOT PASS AGAIN THIS WAY

The bread that bringeth strength I want to give,
The water pure that bids the thirsty live:
I want to help the fainting day by day;
I'm sure I shall not pass again this way.

I want to give the oil of joy for tears,
The faith to conquer crowding doubts and fears.
Beauty for ashes may I give always:
I'm sure I shall not pass again this way.

I want to give good measure running o'er,
And into angry hearts I want to pour
The answer soft that turneth wrath away;
I'm sure I shall not pass again this way.

I want to give to others hope and faith,
I want to do all that the Master saith;
I want to live aright from day to day;
I'm sure I shall not pass again this way.

THE LOWEST EBB

The lowest ebb is the turn of the tide.

Henry Wadsworth Longfellow

THE GOLDEN SIDE

There is many a rest in the road of life.
  If we only would stop to take it,
And many a tone from the better hand,
  If the querulous heart would wake it!
To the sunny soul that is full of hope,
  And whose beautiful trust ne'er faileth,
The grass is green and the flowers are bright,
  Though the wintry storm prevaileth.

Better to hope, though, the clouds hang low,
  And to keep the eyes still lifted;
For the sweet blue sky will soon peep through,
  When the ominous clouds are rifted!
There was never a night without a day,
  Or an evening without a morning,
And the darkest hour, as the proverb goes,
  Is the hour before the dawning.

There is many a gem in the path of life
  Which we pass in our idle pleasure,
That is richer far than the jewelled crown
  Or the miser's hoarded treasure;
It may be the love of a little child,
  Or a mother's prayer to Heaven;
Or only a beggar's grateful thanks
  For a cup of water given.

Better to weave in the web of life
  A bright and golden filling,
And to do God's will with a ready heart
  And hands that are swift and willing,
Than to snap the delicate, slender threads
  Of our curious lives asunder,
And then blame Heaven for the tangled ends,
  And sit and grieve and wonder.

HAIL, SOVEREIGN LOVE

Hail, sovereign love, which first began
The scheme to rescue fallen man!
Hail, matchless, free, eternal grace,
Which gave my soul a Hiding Place.

Against the God who built the sky,
I fought with hands uplifted high,
Despised the mention of His grace,
Too proud to seek a Hiding Place.

Enwrapt in thick Egyptian night,
And fond of darkness more than light,
Madly I ran the sinful race,
Secure, without a Hiding Place.

And thus the eternal counsel ran,
Almighty love, arrest that man!
I felt the arrows of distress,
And found I had no Hiding Place.

Indignant justice stood aview
To Sinai's fiery mount I flew;
But justice cried, with frowning face:
"This mountain is no Hiding Place."

Ere long a heavenly voice I heard,
And Mercy's angel soon appeared;
He led me at a placid pace,
To Jesus as a Hiding Place.

On Him almighty vengeance fell
Which must have sunk a world to Hell.
He bore it for a sinful race,
And thus became their Hiding Place.

Should sevenfold storms of thunder roll,
And shake this globe from pole to pole,
No thunderbolt shall daunt my face,
For Jesus is my Hiding Place.

A few more rolling suns at most,
Shall land me on fair Canaan's coast,
When I shall sing the song of grace,
And see my glorious Hiding Place.

MY GUEST

The day is fixed that there shall come to me
    A strange, mysterious guest;
The time I do not know—he keeps the date—
So all I have to do is work and wait,
    And keep me at my best,
And do my common duties patiently.

I've often wondered if that day would break
    Brighter than other days,
That I might know, or wrapped in some strange
    gloom.
And if he'd find me waiting in my room,
    Or busy with life's ways;
With weary hands and closing eyes that ached.

For many years I've know that he would come,
    And so I've watched for him,
And sometimes even said, "He will come soon,"
Yet mornings pass, followed by afternoon,
    With twilight dusk and dim,
And silent night-times, when the world is dumb,

But he will come, and find me here or there,
    It does not matter where,
For when he comes I know that he will take
In his these very hands of mine that ache
    (They will be idle then)
Just folded, may be, with a silent prayer.

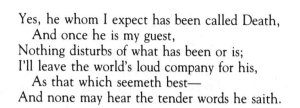

Yes, he whom I expect has been called Death,
    And once he is my guest,
Nothing disturbs of what has been or is;
I'll leave the world's loud company for his,
    As that which seemeth best—
And none may hear the tender words he saith.

As we pass out, my royal guest and I,
    As noiseless as he came,
For naught will do but I must go with him,
And leave the house I've lived in closed and dim,
I've known I should not need it by and by!

And so I sleep and wake, I toil and rest,
    Knowing when he shall come
My Elder Brother will have sent for me,
Bidding him say that they especially
    Have need of me at home;
And so I shall go gladly with my guest.

THERE IS NO DEATH

There is no death! The stars go down
   To rise upon some fairer shore;
And bright in Heaven's jewelled crown
   They shine forevermore.

There is no death! The dust we tread
   Shall change beneath the summer showers,
To golden grain or mellowed fruit,
   Or rainbow-tinted flowers.

The granite rocks disorganize,
   And feed the hungry moss they bear;
The forest leaves drink daily life,
   From out the viewless air.

There is no death! The leaves may fall,
   And flowers may fade and pass away;
They only wait through wintry hours,
   The coming of the May.

There is no death! An angel form
   Walks o'er the earth with silent tread;
He bears our best loved things away;
   And we then call them "dead."

He leaves our hearts all desolate,
   He plucks our fairest, sweetest flowers;
Transplanted into bliss, they now
   Adorn immortal bowers.

The bird-like voice, whose joyous tones,
    Made glad these scenes of sin and strife,
Sings now an everlasting song,
    Around the tree of life.

Where'er He sees a smile too bright,
    Or heart too pure for taint and vice,
He bears it to that world of light,
    To dwell in Paradise.

Born unto that undying life,
    They leave us but to come again;
With joy we welcome them the same—
    Except their sin and pain.

And ever near us, though unseen,
    The dear immortal spirits tread;
For all the boundless universe
    Is life—there are no dead.

WE MEET AT ONE GATE

We meet at one gate
When all's over. The ways they are many and wide,
And seldom are two ways the same. Side by side
May we stand at the same little door when all's
    done.

The ways they are many, the end it is one.
He that knocketh shall enter; who asks shall obtain;
And who seeketh, he findeth.

.   .   .   .

No stream from its source
Flows seaward, how lonely so ever its course,
But what some land is gladdened. No star ever rose
And set without influence somewhere. Who knows
What earth needs from earth's lowest creature? No
    life
Can be pure in its purpose and strong in its strife
And all life not be purer and stronger thereby.
The spirits of just men made perfect on high,
The army of martyrs who stand by the Throne
And gaze into the face that makes glorious their
    own,
Know this, surely at last. Honest love, honest
sorrow,
Honest work for the day, honest hope for the
morrow,
Are these worth nothing more than the hand they
    make weary.

The heart they have saddened, the life they leave
    dreary?
Hush! the sevenfold heavens to the voice of the
    spirit
Echo: "He that o'ercometh shall all things inherit."

Owen Meredith

43

JUST BE GLAD

Oh! heart of mine, we shouldn't worry so!
What we have missed of calm, we couldn't have,
    you know!
    What we have met of stormy pain,
    And of sorrow's driving rain,
    We can better meet again,
        If they blow.

We have erred in that dark hour, we have known;
When the tears fell with the showers, all alone,
    Were not shine and shadow blent
    As the gracious Master meant?
    Let us temper our content
        With His own.

For we know not every morrow can be sad;
So, forgetting all the sorrow we have had,
    Let us fold away our fears
    And put by our foolish tears,
    And through all the coming years,
        Just be glad.

James Whitcomb Riley

THE LAST GATE

"The tomb is but the gateway to an eternity of
opportunity."

THERE ARE LOYAL HEARTS

There are loyal hearts, there are spirits brave,
   There are souls that are pure and true;
Then give to the world the best you have,
   And the best shall come back to you.

Give love, and love to your heart will flow,
   A strength in your utmost need;
Have faith, and a score of hearts will show
   Their faith in your word and deed.

For life is the mirror of king and slave,
   'Tis just what you are and do;
Then give to the world the best you have,
   And the best will come back to you.

UPON THE VALLEY'S LAP

Upon the valley's lap
   The dewy morning throws
A thousand pearly drops
   To wake a single rose.

So, often in the course
   Of life's few fleeting years,
A single pleasure costs
   The soul a thousand tears.

"UNTIL THE DAYBREAK"

A human soul went forth into the night,
   Shutting behind it Death's mysterious door,
And shaking off, with strange, resistless might
     The dust that once it wore.
So swift its flight, so suddenly it sped—
   As when by skillful hand a bow is bent
The arrow flies—those watching round the bed
     Marked not the way it went.

Heavy with grief, their aching, tear-dimmed eyes
   Saw but the shadow fall, and knew not when,
Or in what fair or unfamiliar guise,
     It left the world of men.
It broke from sickness, that with iron bands
   Had bound it fast for many a grievous day;
And love itself with its restraining hands
     Might not its course delay.

Space could not hold it back with fettering bars,
   Time lost its power, and ceased at last to be;
It swept beyond the boundary of the stars,
     And touched Eternity.
Out from the house of mourning faintly lit,
   It passed upon its journey all alone;
So far not even thought could follow it
     Into those realms unknown.

Through the clear silence of the moonless dark,
    Leaving no footprint of the road it trod,
Straight as an arrow cleaving to its mark,
        The soul went home to God.
"Alas!" they cried, "he never saw the morn,
    But fell asleep outwearied with the strife"—
Nay, rather, he arose and met the dawn
        Of Everlasting Life.

SOMETIME

"What I do thou knowest not now, but thou shalt
know hereafter."

Sometime, when all life's lessons have been learned,
    And sun and stars forevermore have set,
The things which our weak judgment here have
    spurned,
The things o'er which we grieved with lashes wet,
Will flash before us, out of life's dark night,
    As stars shine more in deeper tints of blue,
And we shall see how all God's plans were right,
    And how what seemed reproof was love most
    true.

And we shall see how, while we frown and sigh,
    God's plans go on as best for you and me;
How, when we called, He heeded not our cry,
    Because His wisdom to the end could see.
And even as prudent parents disallow
    Too much of sweet to craving babyhood,
So God, perhaps, is keeping from us now
    Life's sweetest things, because it seemeth good.

And if, sometimes commingled with life's wine,
    We find the wormwood and rebel and shrink,
Be sure a wiser hand than yours or mine
    Pours out this potion for our lips to drink.

And if some friend we love is lying low,
  Where human kisses cannot reach his face,
Oh, do not blame the loving Father so!
  But wear your sorrow with obedient grace.

And you shall shortly know that lengthened breath
  Is not the sweetest gift God sends His friend,
And that sometimes the sable pall of death
  Conceals the fairest boon His love can send.
If we could push ajar the gates of life
  And stand within and all God's workings see,
We could interpret all this doubt and strife,
  And for each mystery could find a key.

But not today. Then be content, poor heart!
  God's plans, like lilies, pure and white unfold.
We must not tear the close-shut leaves apart;
  Time will reveal the hidden cups of gold,
And if through patient toil we reach the land,
  Where weary feet, with sandals loosed, may rest,
Then shall we know and clearly understand—
  I think that we shall say, "God knew the best."

THE CREATOR IN CREATION

I am the mote in the sunbeam, and I am the burning
 sun;
"Rest here!" I whisper the atom; I call to the orb,
 "Roll on!"
I am the blush of morning, and I am the evening
 breeze,
I am the leaf's low murmur, the swell of the terrible
 seas.
I am the net, the fowler, the bird and its frightened
 cry,
The mirror, the form reflected, the sound and its
 echo, I;
The lover's passionate pleading, the maiden's
 whispered fear,
The warrior, the blade that smites him, his mother's
 heartwrung tear.
I am intoxication, grapes, wine-press, and must,
 and wine,
The guest, the host, the tavern, the goblet of crystal
 fine;
I am the breath of the flute, and I am the mind
 of man,
Gold's glitter, the light of the diamond, the sea
 pearl's lustre wan;
The rose, her poet nightingale, the songs from his
 throat that rise,
Flint sparks, the flame, the taper, the moth that
 about it flies.
I am both Good and Evil; the deed, and deed's
 intent,

50

Temptation, victim, sinner, crime, pardon and
    punishment;
I am what was, is, will be; creation's ascent and
    fall;
The link, the chain of existence; beginning and
    end of All!

THE CHOIR INVISIBLE

O may I join the choir invisible
Of those immortal dead who live again
In minds made better by their presence; live
In pulses stirred to generosity,
In deeds of daring rectitude, in scorn
For miserable aims that end with self,
In thoughts sublime that pierce the night like stars,
And with their mild persistence urge man's search
To vaster issues.
            So to live is Heaven;
To make undying music in the world,
Breathing as beauteous order that controls
With growing sway the growing life of man.
So we inherit that sweet purity
For which we struggled, failed and agonized
With widening retrospect that bred despair.
Rebellious flesh that would not be subdued,
A vicious parent shaming still its child,
Poor anxious penitence is quick dissolved;
Its discords, quenched by meeting harmonies,
Die in the large and charitable air.
And all our rarer, better, truer self,
That sobbed religiously in yearning song,
That watched to ease the burden of the world,
Laboriously tracing what must be,
And what may yet be better—saw within
A worthier image for the sanctuary,
And shaped it forth before the multitude
Divinely human, raising worship so

To higher reverence more mixed with love—
That better self shall live till human Time
Shall fold its eyelids, and the human sky
Be gathered like a scroll within the tomb
Unread forever.
                    This is life to come,
Which martyred men have made more glorious
For us who strive to follow. May I reach
That purest heaven, be to other souls
The cup of strength in some great agony,
Enkindle generous ardor, feed pure love,
Beget the smiles that have no cruelty—
Be the sweet presence of a good diffused,
And in diffusion ever more intense.
So shall I join the choir invisible
Whose music is the gladness of the world.

George Eliot

53

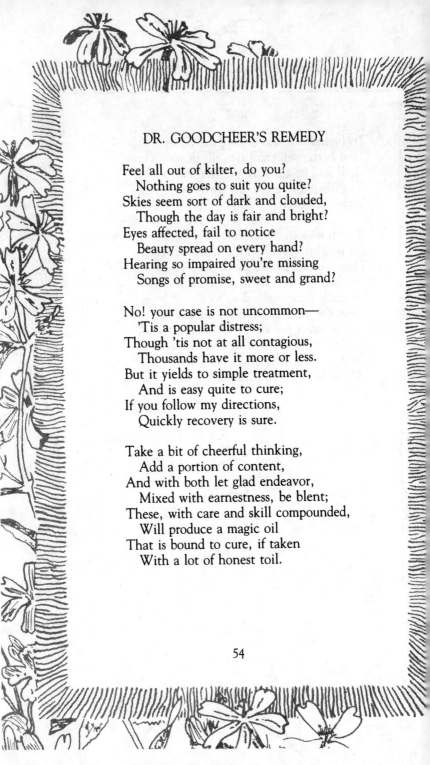

DR. GOODCHEER'S REMEDY

Feel all out of kilter, do you?
    Nothing goes to suit you quite?
Skies seem sort of dark and clouded,
    Though the day is fair and bright?
Eyes affected, fail to notice
    Beauty spread on every hand?
Hearing so impaired you're missing
    Songs of promise, sweet and grand?

No! your case is not uncommon—
    'Tis a popular distress;
Though 'tis not at all contagious,
    Thousands have it more or less.
But it yields to simple treatment,
    And is easy quite to cure;
If you follow my directions,
    Quickly recovery is sure.

Take a bit of cheerful thinking,
    Add a portion of content,
And with both let glad endeavor,
    Mixed with earnestness, be blent;
These, with care and skill compounded,
    Will produce a magic oil
That is bound to cure, if taken
    With a lot of honest toil.

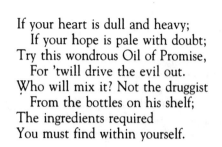

If your heart is dull and heavy;
  If your hope is pale with doubt;
Try this wondrous Oil of Promise,
  For 'twill drive the evil out.
Who will mix it? Not the druggist
  From the bottles on his shelf;
The ingredients required
You must find within yourself.

RECESSIONAL

God of our fathers, known of old—
    Lord of our far-flung battle-line—
Beneath whose awful hand we hold
    Dominion over palm and pine—
Lord God of Hosts, be with us yet,
Lest we forget—lest we forget!

The tumult and the shouting dies—
    The captains and the kings depart—
Still stands Thine ancient Sacrifice,
    An humble and a contrite heart.
Lord God of Hosts, be with us yet,
Lest we forget—lest we forget!

Far-called our navies melt away—
    On dune and headline sinks the fire—
Lo, all our pomp of yesterday
    Is one with Nineveh and Tyre!
Judge of the Nations, spare us yet,
Lest we forget—lest we forget!

If, drunk with sight of power, we loose
    Wild tongues that have not Thee in awe—
Such boasting as the Gentiles use
    Or lesser breeds without the Law—
Lord God of Hosts, be with us yet,
Lest we forget—lest we forget!

For heathen heart that puts her trust
  In reeking tube and iron shard—
All valiant dust that builds on dust,
  And guarding calls not Thee to guard—
For frantic boast and foolish word,
Thy Mercy on Thy People, Lord!

                              Amen.

Rudyard Kipling

NEARER, MY GOD, TO THEE

Nearer, my God, to Thee,
  Nearer to Thee!
E'en though it be a cross
  That raiseth me;
Still all my song shall be,
Nearer, my God, to Thee,
  Nearer to Thee!

Though like the wanderer,
  The sun gone down,
Darkness be over me,
  My rest a stone;
Yet in my dreams I'd be
Nearer, my God, to Thee,
  Nearer to Thee!

There let the way appear,
  Steps unto heaven;
All that Thou sendest me
  In mercy given;
Angels to beckon me
Nearer, my God, to Thee,
  Nearer to Thee!

Then, with my waking thoughts
  Bright with Thy praise,
Out of my stony griefs,
  Bethel I'll raise
So by my woes to be

Nearer, my God, to Thee,
    Nearer to Thee!

Or if, on joyful wing,
    Cleaving the sky,
Sun, moon and stars forgot,
    Upward I fly;
Still all my song shall be,
Nearer, my God, to Thee,
    Nearer to Thee!

HOW DID YOU DIE?

Did you tackle the trouble that came your way
    With a resolute heart and cheerful?
Or hide your face from the light of day
    With a craven soul and fearful?
Oh, a trouble's a ton, or a trouble's an ounce,
    Or a trouble is what you make it,
And it isn't the fact that you're hurt that counts,
    But only how did you take it?

You are beaten to earth? Well, well, what's that?
    Come up with a smiling face.
It's nothing against you to fall down flat,
    But to lie there—that's disgrace.
The harder you're thrown, why, the higher you
        bounce;
    Be proud of your blackened eye!
It isn't the fact that you're licked that counts;
    It's how did you fight—and why?

And though you be done to the death, what then?
    If you battled the best you could,
If you played your part in the world of men,
    Why, the Critic will call it good.
Death comes with a crawl, or comes with a pounce,
    And whether he's slow or spry,
It isn't the fact that you're dead that counts,
    But only how did you die?

WE SEE WITH OUR VISION IMPERFECT

We see with our vision imperfect,
    Such causes of dread or fear,
Some that are far in the distance,
    And some that may never be near;
When if we would trust in His wisdom,
    Whose purpose we cannot see,
We would find, whatever our trial,
    As our day, our strength shall be.

ON THE TWENTY-THIRD PSALM

In "pastures green"? Not always; sometimes He
Who knoweth best, in kindness leadeth me
In weary ways, where heavy shadows be.

And by "still waters"? No, not always so;
Oft-times the heavy tempests round me blow.
And o'er my soul the waves and billows go.

But when the storms beat loudest, and I cry
Aloud for help, the Master standeth by,
And whispers to my soul, "Lo, it is I!"

So, where He leads me, I can safely go.
And in the blest hereafter I shall know
Why, in His wisdom, He had led me so.

61

JESUS, LOVER OF MY SOUL

Jesus, Lover of my soul,
  Let me to Thy bosom fly,
While the nearer waters roll,
  While the tempest still is high;
Hide me, O my Saviour, hide
  Till the storm of life is past;
Safe into the haven guide,
  O receive my soul at last.

Other refuge have I none;
  Hangs my helpless soul on Thee;
Leave, ah! leave me not alone,
  Still support and comfort me.
All my trust on Thee is stayed,
  All my help from Thee I bring;
Cover my defenceless head
  With the shadow of Thy wing.

Wilt Thou not regard my call?
  Wilt Thou not accept my prayer?
Lo, I sink, I faint, I fall!
  Lo, on Thee I cast my care;
Reach me out Thy gracious hand!
  While I of Thy strength receive,
Hoping against hope I stand,
  Dying, and behold I live!

Thou, O Christ, art all I want;
   More than all in Thee I find;
Raise the fallen, cheer the faint,
   Heal the sick and lead the blind.
Just and holy is Thy name;
   I am all unrighteousness;
False and full of sin I am,
   Thou art full of truth and grace.

Plenteous grace with Thee is found,
   Grace to cover all my sin;
Let the healing streams abound,
   Make and keep me pure within.
Thou of life the Fountain art,
   Freely let me take of Thee;
Spring Thou up within my heart,
   Rise to all eternity.

Charles Wesley

A PSALM OF LIFE

Tell me not in mournful numbers,
    "Life is but an empty dream!"
For the soul is dead that slumbers,
    And things are not what they seem.

Life is real! Life is earnest!
    And the grave is not its goal;
"Dust thou art, to dust returnest,"
    Was not spoken of the soul.

Not enjoyment and not sorrow,
    Is our destined end or way;
But to act, that each tomorrow
    Find us farther than today.

Art is long, and time is fleeting,
    And our hearts, though stout and brave,
Still, like muffled drums are beating
    Funeral marches to the grave.

In the world's broad field of battle,
    In the bivouac of life,
Be not like dumb, driven cattle!
    Be a hero in the strife!

Trust no future, howe'er pleasant!
    Let the dead past bury its dead!
Act, act in the living present!
    Heart within and God o'erhead!

64

Lives of great men all remind us
   We can make our lives sublime,
And, departing, leave behind us
   Footprints on the sands of time.

Footprints, that perhaps another,
   Sailing o'er life's solemn main,
A forlorn and shipwrecked brother,
   Seeing, shall take heart again.

Let us, then, be up and doing,
   With a heart for any fate;
Still achieving, still pursuing,
   Learn to labor and to wait.

Henry W. Longfellow

BEREAVED

Let me come in where you sit weeping—aye
Let me, who have not any child to die,
Weep with you for the little one whose love
I have known nothing of.

The little arms that slowly, slowly loosed
Their pressure round your neck; the hands you used
To kiss—such arms, such hands I never knew,
May I not weep with you?

Fain would I be of service—say something,
Between the tears, that would be comforting—
But ah! so sadder than yourself am I
Who have no child to die!

James Whitcomb Riley

WHO NE'ER HAS SUFFERED

Who ne'er has suffered, he has lived but half.
  Who never failed, he never strove or sought.
Who never wept is stranger to a laugh.
  And he who never doubted never thought.

LEAVES OF INSPIRATION

FOREWORD

"If you have built castles in the air,
Your work need not be lost;
That is where they should be.
Now put foundations under them."
Henry David Thoreau

The quotations gathered in *Leaves of Inspiration* are a unique collection, featuring the wisdom of great writers—Robert Louis Stevenson, Abraham Lincoln, Henry David Thoreau, Henry Van Dyke, Leonardo da Vinci, William Shakespeare, Sir Walter Scott and others. But the anonymous writer, the "little person," is also represented in this collection, each one revealing his original and sensitive insights into life.

The humdrum details of daily living can dull our senses and blind us to the full beauty and potential of life. Between earning a living, paying bills, running errands and just keeping body and soul together, we often feel as if we have no time or energy to realize our full potential as human beings or to develop our personal talents and gifts.

The quotations gathered here give us that extra push to achieve our goals; they remind us that an act of love, however small, enriches our life immeasurably. The authors quoted here were also people with too much to do, who at times undoubtedly felt overburdened and depressed by life.

But their gift was their ability to stop and recognize their true priorities, to show us that working toward a dream and caring for the people around us makes life a wonderful experience, not a drudgery to be endured.

These quotations motivate and encourage us; they lift our spirits after a hard day or an upsetting experience. By drawing us out of our self-absorption, *Leaves of Inspiration* shows us how delightful life is, how much happiness we can achieve if we not only build castles in the air but work at putting foundations under them.

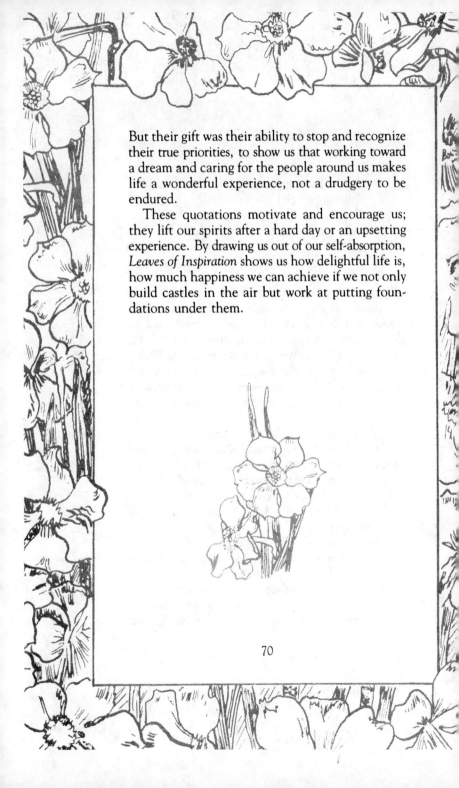

IF YOU HAVE BUILT CASTLES IN THE AIR

If you have built castles in the air,
Your work need not be lost;
that is where they should be.
Now put foundations under them.

Henry David Thoreau

FOR THOSE WHO FAIL

"All honor to him who shall win the prize,"
The world has cried for a thousand years,
But to him who tries and who fails and dies,
I give great honor and glory and tears.

Give glory and honor and pitiful tears
To all who fail in their deeds sublime,
Their ghosts are many in the van of years,
They were born with Time in advance of Time.

Oh, great is the hero who wins a name,
But greater many and many a time
Some pale-faced fellow who dies in shame
And lets God finish the thought sublime.

And great is the man with a sword undrawn,
And good is the man who refrains from wine;
But the man who fails and who still fights on,
Lo, he is the twin-brother of mine.

71

LET SOMETHING GOOD BE SAID

When over the fair fame of friend or foe
   The shadow of disgrace shall fall; instead
Of words of blame, or proof of so and so,
   Let something good be said.

Forget not that no fellow-being yet
   May fall so low but love may lift his head;
Even the cheek of shame with tears is wet,
   If something good be said.

No generous heart may vainly turn aside
   In ways of sympathy; no soul so dead
But may awaken strong and glorified,
   If something good be said.

And so I charge ye, by the thorny crown,
   And by the cross on which the Saviour bled,
And by your own soul's hope for fair renown,
   Let something good be said.

James Whitcomb Riley

LOOK UP!

Look up! and not down;
Out! and not in;
Forward! and not back;
And lend a hand.

72

THE FOOTPATH TO PEACE

To be glad of life, because it gives you the chance to love and to work and to play and to look up at the stars; to be satisfied with your possessions, but not contented with yourself until you have made the best of them; to despise nothing in the world except falsehood and meanness, and to fear nothing except cowardice; to be governed by your admirations rather than by your disgusts; to covet nothing that is your neighbor's except his kindness of heart and gentleness of manners; to think seldom of your enemies, often of your friends and every day of Christ; and to spend as much time as you can with body and with spirit, in God's out-of-doors—these are little guide-posts on the footpath to peace.

Henry Van Dyke

THANK GOD EVERY MORNING

Thank God every morning when you get up that you have something to do that day which must be done, whether you like it or not. Being forced to work, and forced to do your best, will breed in you temperance and self-control, diligence and strength of will, cheerfulness and content, and a hundred virtues which the idle never know.

73

THE WONDROUS CROSS

When I survey the wondrous cross
   On which the Prince of Glory died,
My richest gain I count but loss,
   And pour contempt on all my pride.

Forbid it, Lord! that I should boast,
   Save in the death of Christ, my God;
All the vain things that charm me most
   I sacrifice them to His blood.

See, from His head, His hands, His feet,
   Sorrow and love flow mingled down;
Did e'er such love and sorrows meet,
   Or thorns compose so rich a crown?

His dying crimson, like a robe,
   Spreads o'er His body on the tree;
Then I am dead to all the globe,
   And all the globe is dead to me.

Were the whole realm of nature mine,
   That were a present far too small;
Love so amazing, so divine,
   Demands my soul, my life, my all.

Isaac Watts

GIVE THEM THE FLOWERS NOW

Closed eyes can't see the white roses,
  Cold hands can't hold them, you know,
Breath that is stilled cannot gather
  The odors that sweet from them blow.
Death, with a peace beyond dreaming,
  Its children of earth doth endow;
Life is the time we can help them,
  So give them the flowers now!

Here are the struggles and striving,
  Here are the cares and the tears;
Now is the time to be smoothing
  The frowns and the furrows and fears.
What to closed eyes are kind sayings?
  What to hushed heart is deep vow?
Naught can avail after parting,
  So give them the flowers now!

GREAT MINDS

Great minds have purposes; little minds have
wishes. Little minds are subdued by misfortunes;
great minds rise above them.

Washington Irving

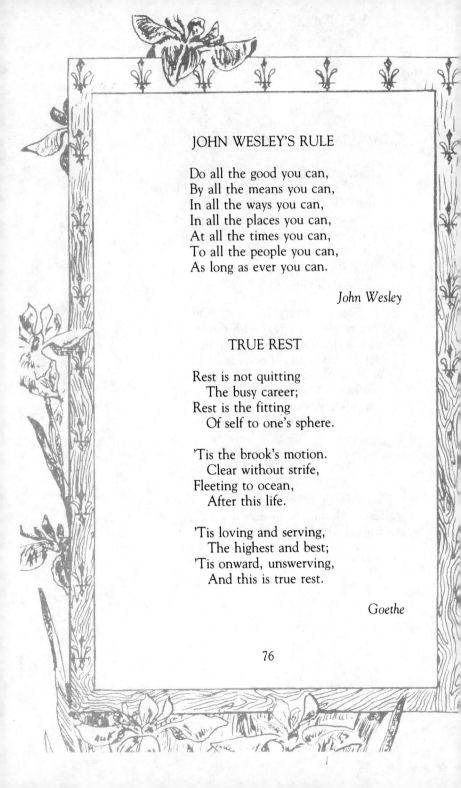

JOHN WESLEY'S RULE

Do all the good you can,
By all the means you can,
In all the ways you can,
In all the places you can,
At all the times you can,
To all the people you can,
As long as ever you can.

John Wesley

TRUE REST

Rest is not quitting
   The busy career;
Rest is the fitting
   Of self to one's sphere.

'Tis the brook's motion.
   Clear without strife,
Fleeting to ocean,
   After this life.

'Tis loving and serving,
   The highest and best;
'Tis onward, unswerving,
   And this is true rest.

Goethe

SUCCESS

Trifles make perfection, but perfection is no trifle.

Michelangelo

The word "success" appears but once in the Bible, in the following verse:

This book of the law shall not depart out of thy mouth; but thou shalt meditate therein day and night, that thou mayest observe to do according to all that is written therein: for then thou shalt make thy way prosperous, and then thou shalt have good success.

Joshua 1: 8

A ROSE TO THE LIVING

A rose to the living is more
   Than sumptuous wreaths to the dead;
In filling love's infinite store,
A rose to the living is more
If graciously given before
   The hungering spirit is fled—
A rose to the living is more
   Than sumptuous wreaths to the dead.

ONE HOUR OF LIFE

One hour of life, crowded to the full with glorious action, and filled with noble risks, is worth whole years of those mean observances of petty decorum, in which men steal through existence, like sluggish waters through a marsh, without either honor or observation.

Sir Walter Scott

FAME

The heights by great men reached and kept
  Were not attained by sudden flight,
But they while their companions slept
  Were toiling upward in the night.

Henry W. Longfellow

SPANISH PROVERB

The pleasures of the senses pass quickly; those of the heart become sorrows, but those of the mind are ever with us, even to the end of our journey.

LITTLE BY LITTLE

Little by little the time goes by—
Short, if you sing through it, long, if you sigh,
Little by little—an hour a day,
Gone with the years that have vanished away.
Little by little the race is run;
Trouble and waiting and toil are done!

Little by little the skies grow clear;
Little by little the sun comes near;
Little by little the days smile out,
Gladder and brighter on pain and doubt;
Little by little the seed we sow
Into a beautiful yield will grow.

Little by little the world grows strong,
Fighting the battle of Right and Wrong;
Little by little the Wrong gives way—
Little by little the Right has sway.
Little by little all longing souls
Struggle up nearer the shining goals.

Little by little the good in men
Blossoms to beauty, for human ken;
Little by little the angels see
Prophecies better of good to be;
Little by little the God of all
Lifts the world nearer the pleading call.

IS IT WORTH WHILE?

Is it worth while that we jostle a brother,
   Bearing his load on the rough road of life?
Is it worth while that we jeer at each other—
   In blackness of heart, that we war to the knife?
   God pity us all in our pitiful strife.

God pity us all as we jostle each other;
   God pardon us all for the triumph we feel
When a fellow goes down 'neath his load on the
     heather,
   Pierced to the heart: Words are keener than steel,
   And mightier far for woe than for weal.

Were it not well, in this brief little journey
   On over the isthmus, down into the tide,
We give him a fish instead of a serpent,
   Ere folding the hands to be and abide
   Forever and aye in dust at his side?

Look at the roses saluting each other;
   Look at the herds all at peace on the plain;
Man, and man only, makes war on his brother,
   And laughs in his heart at his peril and pain—
   Shamed by the beasts that go down on the plain.

Is it worth while that we battle to humble
  Some poor fellow down into the dust?
God pity us all! Time too soon will tumble
  All of us together, like leaves in a gust,
  Humbled, indeed, down into the dust.

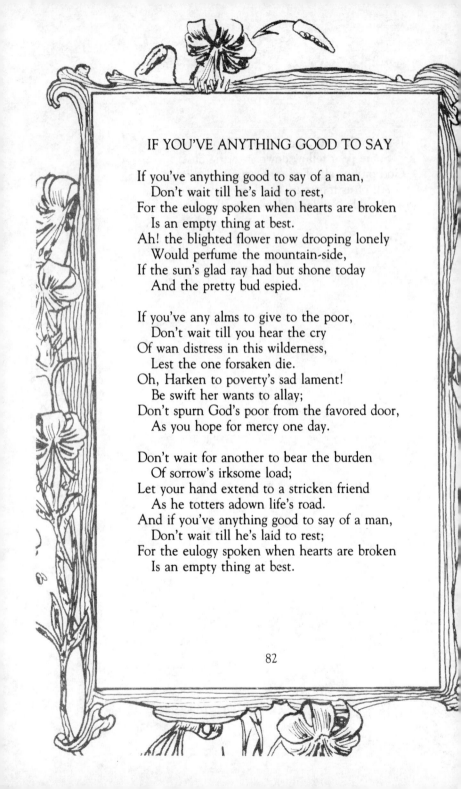

IF YOU'VE ANYTHING GOOD TO SAY

If you've anything good to say of a man,
   Don't wait till he's laid to rest,
For the eulogy spoken when hearts are broken
   Is an empty thing at best.
Ah! the blighted flower now drooping lonely
   Would perfume the mountain-side,
If the sun's glad ray had but shone today
   And the pretty bud espied.

If you've any alms to give to the poor,
   Don't wait till you hear the cry
Of wan distress in this wilderness,
   Lest the one forsaken die.
Oh, Harken to poverty's sad lament!
   Be swift her wants to allay;
Don't spurn God's poor from the favored door,
   As you hope for mercy one day.

Don't wait for another to bear the burden
   Of sorrow's irksome load;
Let your hand extend to a stricken friend
   As he totters adown life's road.
And if you've anything good to say of a man,
   Don't wait till he's laid to rest;
For the eulogy spoken when hearts are broken
   Is an empty thing at best.

LET US SMILE

The thing that goes the farthest towards making
    life worth while,
That costs the least and does the most, is just a
    pleasant smile,
The smile that bubbles from a heart that loves its
    fellowmen
Will drive away the cloud of gloom and coax the
    sun again,
It's full of worth and goodness, too, with manly
    kindness blent—
It's worth a million dollars, and doesn't cost a cent.

CHARITY

There is so much that is bad in the best of us
And so much that is good in the worst of us
That it doesn't behoove any of us
To talk about the rest of us.

DO IT NOW

I expect to pass through this world but once.
Any good thing, therefore, that I can do or any
kindness I can show to any fellow human being
let me do it now. Let me not defer nor neglect it,
for I shall not pass this way again.

83

SHAKESPEARE'S WISDOM

And these few precepts in thy memory
See thou character. Give thy thoughts no tongue,
Nor any unproportioned thought his act.
Be thou familiar, but by no means vulgar.
Those friends thou hast, and their adoption tried,
Grapple them to thy soul with hoops of steel,
But do not dull thy palm with entertainment
Of each new-hatched unfledged comrade. Beware
of entrance to a quarrel; but being in,
Bear't, that the opposed may beware of thee.
Give every man thy ear, but few thy voice:
Take each man's censure, but reserve thy judgment.
Costly thy habit as thy purse can buy,
But not expressed in fancy; rich, not gaudy:
For the apparel oft proclaims the man;
And they in France of the best rank and station
Are of a most select and generous chief in that.
Neither a borrower nor a lender be:
For loan oft loses both itself and friend,
And borrowing dulls the edge of husbandry.
This above all: to thine own self be true,
And it must follow, as the night the day,
Thou canst not then be false to any man.

William Shakespeare

SPEAK GENTLY

Speak gently; it is better far
  To rule by love than fear;
Speak gently; let no harsh word mar
  The good we may do here.
Speak gently to the little child;
  Its love is sure to gain;
Teach it in accents soft and mild;
  It may not long remain.

Speak gently to the young, for they
  Will have enough to bear;
Pass through this life as best they may,
  'Tis full of anxious care,
Speak gently to the aged one,
  Grieve not the careworn heart,
Whose sands of life are nearly run:
  Let such in peace depart.

Speak gently to the erring; know
  They must have toiled in vain;
Perchance unkindness made them so;
  Oh, win them back again!
Speak gently; 'tis a little thing
  Dropped in the heart's deep well;
The good, the joy, that it may bring,
  Eternity shall tell.

FOR ALL THESE

I thank Thee, Lord, that I am straight and strong,
    With wit to work and hope to keep me brave;
That two score years, unfathomed, still belong
    To the allotted life Thy bounty gave.

I thank Thee that the sight of sunlit lands
    And dipping hills, the breath of evening grass—
That wet, dark rocks and flowers in my hands
    Can give me daily gladness as I pass.

I thank Thee that I love the things of Earth—
    Ripe fruits and laughter, lying down to sleep,
The shine of lighted towns, the graver worth
    Of beating human hearts that laugh and weep.

I thank Thee that as yet I need not know,
    Yet need not fear the mystery of end:
But more than all, and though all these should go—
    Dear Lord, this on my knees!—I thank Thee for
my friend.

FRIENDSHIP

So long as we love, we serve. So long as we are
loved by others I would almost say we were indis-
pensable; and no man is useless while he has a
friend.

Robert Louis Stevenson

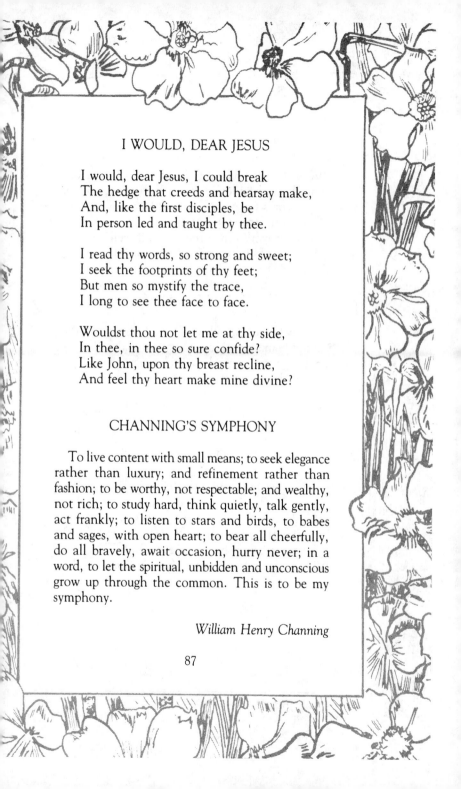

I WOULD, DEAR JESUS

I would, dear Jesus, I could break
The hedge that creeds and hearsay make,
And, like the first disciples, be
In person led and taught by thee.

I read thy words, so strong and sweet;
I seek the footprints of thy feet;
But men so mystify the trace,
I long to see thee face to face.

Wouldst thou not let me at thy side,
In thee, in thee so sure confide?
Like John, upon thy breast recline,
And feel thy heart make mine divine?

CHANNING'S SYMPHONY

To live content with small means; to seek elegance
rather than luxury; and refinement rather than
fashion; to be worthy, not respectable; and wealthy,
not rich; to study hard, think quietly, talk gently,
act frankly; to listen to stars and birds, to babes
and sages, with open heart; to bear all cheerfully,
do all bravely, await occasion, hurry never; in a
word, to let the spiritual, unbidden and unconscious
grow up through the common. This is to be my
symphony.

William Henry Channing

WORK THOU FOR PLEASURE

Work thou for pleasure; paint or sing or carve
The thing thou lovest, though the body starve.
Who works for glory misses oft the goal;
Who works for money coins his very soul.
Work for work's sake then, and it well may be
That these things shall be added unto thee.

THANKFULNESS

Many favours which God giveth us ravel out for
want of hemming, through our own unthankfulness;
for though prayer purchaseth blessings, giving praise
doth keep the quiet possession of them.

Thomas Fuller

PLUCK WINS

Pluck wins! It always wins! though days be slow
And nights be dark 'twixt days that come and go.
Still pluck will win; its average is sure;
He gains the prize who will the most endure;
Who faces issues; he who never shirks;
Who waits and watches, and who always works.

WHAT HAVE WE DONE TODAY?

We shall do so much in the years to come,
    But what have we done today?
We shall give our gold in a princely sum,
    But what did we give today?
We shall lift the heart and dry the tear,
We shall plant a hope in the place of fear,
We shall speak the words of love and cheer,
    But what did we speak today?

We shall be so kind in the afterwhile,
    But what have we been today?
We shall bring each lonely life a smile,
    But what have we brought today?
We shall give to truth a grander birth,
And to steadfast faith a deeper worth,
We shall feed the hungering souls of earth,
    But whom have we fed today?

We shall reap such joys in the by and by,
    But what have we sown today?
We shall build us mansions in the sky,
    But what have we built today?
'Tis sweet in idle dreams to bask,
But here and now do we do our task?
Yes, this is the thing our souls must ask,
    "What have we done today?"

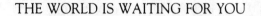

THE WORLD IS WAITING FOR YOU

The world is waiting for you, young man,
    If your purpose is strong and true;
If out of your treasures of mind and heart,
    You can bring things old and new,
If you know the truth that makes men free,
    And with skill can bring it to view,
The world is waiting for you, young man,
    The world is waiting for you.

There are treasures of mountain and treasures of
        sea,
    And harvest of valley and plain,
That Industry, Knowledge and Skill can secure,
    While Ignorance wishes in vain.
To scatter the lightning and harness the storm,
    Is a power that is wielded by few;
If you have the nerve and the skill, young man,
    The world is waiting for you.

Of the idle and brainless the world has enough—
    Who eat what they never have earned;
Who hate the pure stream from the fountain of
        truth,
    And wisdom and knowledge have spurned.
But patience and purpose which know no defeat,
    And genius like gems bright and true,
Will bless all mankind with their love, life and
        light,—
    The world is waiting for you.

Then awake, O young man, from the stupor of
    doubt
  And prepare for the battle of life;
Be the fire of the forge, or be anvil or sledge,—
  But win, or go down in the strife!
Can you stand though the world into ruin should
    rock?
  Can you conquer with many or few?
Then the world is waiting for you, young man,
  The world is waiting for you!

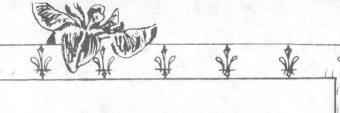

THE SAYING OF OMAR IBN AL HALIF

The Second Caliph

Four things come not back:
The spoken word;
The sped arrow;
Time past;
The neglected opportunity.

TODAY!

With every rising of the sun
Think of your life as just begun.

The Past has cancelled and buried deep
All yesterdays. There let them sleep.

Concern yourself with but Today.
Grasp it, and teach it to obey

Your will and plan. Since time began
Today has been the friend of man.

You and Today! A soul sublime
And the great heritage of time.

With God himself to bind the twain,
Go forth, brave heart! Attain! attain!

BE STRONG!

Be strong!
We are not here to play—to dream, to drift.
We have hard work to do and loads to lift.
Shun not the struggle—face it; 'tis God's gift.

Be strong!
Say not the days are evil. Who's to blame?
And fold the hands and acquiesce—O shame!
Stand up, speak out, and bravely, in God's name.

Be strong!
It matters not how deep intrenched the wrong,
How hard the battle goes, the day how long;
Faint not—fight on! Tomorrow comes the song.

WHAT OTHERS MAY NOT SEE!

If each man's secret, unguessed care
    Were written on his brow,
How many would our pity share
    Who have our envy now!
And if the promptings of each heart
    No artifice concealed,
How many trusting friends would part
    At what they saw revealed!

CONSEQUENCES

A traveler on a dusty road
  Strewed acorns on the lea;
And one took root and sprouted up,
  And grew into a tree.
Love sought its shade at evening time,
  To breathe his early vows.
And age was pleased, in heats of noon
  To bask beneath its boughs;
The dormouse loved its dangling twigs,
  The birds sweet music bore;
It stood a glory in its place,
  A blessing evermore.

A little spring had lost its way
  Amid the grass and fern;
A passing stranger scooped a well
  Where weary men might turn.
He walled it in, and hung with care
  A ladle at the brink;
He thought not of the deed he did,
  But judged that all might drink.
He paused again, and lo! the well,
  By summer never dried,
Had cooled ten thousand parching tongues
  And saved a life beside.

A dreamer dropped a random thought;
  'Twas old, and yet 'twas new;
A simple fancy of the brain,
  But strong in being true.

It shone upon a genial mind,
   And lo! its light became
A lamp of life, a beacon ray,
   A monitory flame.
The thought was small, its issue great;
   A watch-fire on the hill;
It shed its radiance far adown,
   And cheers the valley still.

A nameless man, amid a crowd
   That thronged the daily mart,
Let fall a word of Hope and Love,
   Unstudied from the heart;
A whisper on the tumult thrown,
   A transitory breath—
It raised a brother from the dust,
   It saved a soul from death.
O germ! O fount! O word of love!
   O thought at random cast!
Ye were but little at the first,
   But mighty at the last.

HULLO!

When you see a man in woe,
Walk straight up and say, "Hullo!"
Say, "Hullo!" and "How d'ye do?
How's the world been using you?"
Slap the fellow on his back,
Bring your hand down with a whack;
Waltz straight up and don't go slow,
Shake his hand and say, "Hullo!"

Is he clothed in rags? Oh, ho!
Walk straight up and say, "Hullo!"
Rags are but a cotton roll
Just for wrapping up a soul;
And a soul is worth a true
Hale and hearty "How d'ye do?"
Don't wait for the crowd to go;
Walk straight up and say, "Hullo!"

When big vessels meet, they say,
They salute and sail away:
Just the same as you and me,
Lonely ships upon the sea,
Each one sailing his own jog
For a port beyond the fog;
Let your speaking-trumpet blow,
Lift your horn and cry, "Hullo!"

Say "Hullo!" and "How d'ye do?"
Other folks are good as you.
When you leave your house of clay,
Wandering in the far away;
When you travel through the strange
Country far beyond the range,
Then the souls you've cheered will know
Who you be, and say, "Hullo!"

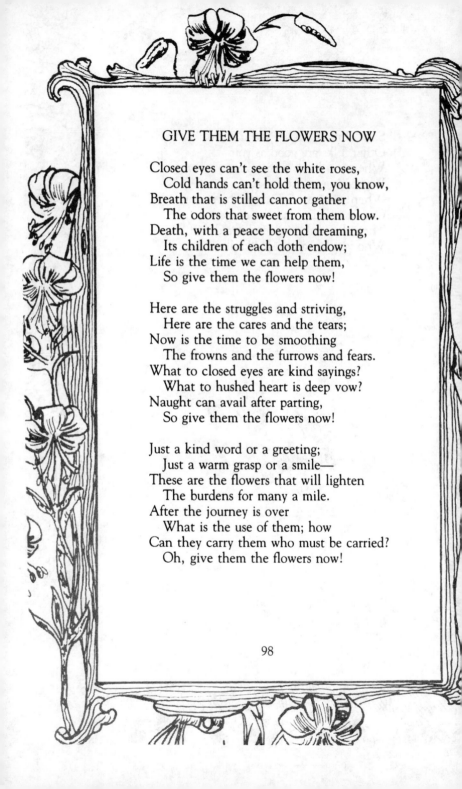

GIVE THEM THE FLOWERS NOW

Closed eyes can't see the white roses,
  Cold hands can't hold them, you know,
Breath that is stilled cannot gather
  The odors that sweet from them blow.
Death, with a peace beyond dreaming,
  Its children of each doth endow;
Life is the time we can help them,
  So give them the flowers now!

Here are the struggles and striving,
  Here are the cares and the tears;
Now is the time to be smoothing
  The frowns and the furrows and fears.
What to closed eyes are kind sayings?
  What to hushed heart is deep vow?
Naught can avail after parting,
  So give them the flowers now!

Just a kind word or a greeting;
  Just a warm grasp or a smile—
These are the flowers that will lighten
  The burdens for many a mile.
After the journey is over
  What is the use of them; how
Can they carry them who must be carried?
  Oh, give them the flowers now!

Blooms from the happy heart's garden
 Plucked in the spirit of love;
Blooms that are earthly reflections
 Of flowers that blossom above.
Words cannot tell what a measure
 Of blessings such gifts will allow
To dwell in the lives of many,
 So give them the flowers now!

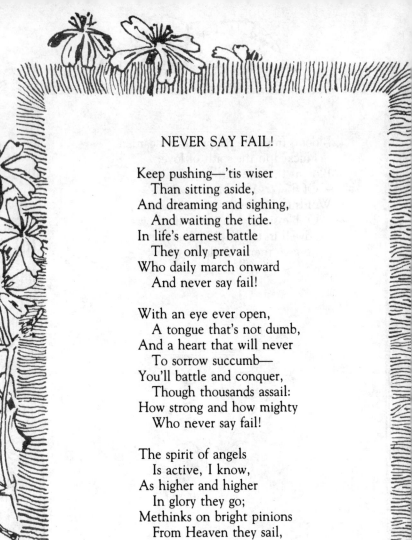

NEVER SAY FAIL!

Keep pushing—'tis wiser
   Than sitting aside,
And dreaming and sighing,
   And waiting the tide.
In life's earnest battle
   They only prevail
Who daily march onward
   And never say fail!

With an eye ever open,
   A tongue that's not dumb,
And a heart that will never
   To sorrow succumb—
You'll battle and conquer,
   Though thousands assail:
How strong and how mighty
   Who never say fail!

The spirit of angels
   Is active, I know,
As higher and higher
   In glory they go;
Methinks on bright pinions
   From Heaven they sail,
To cheer and encourage
   Who never say fail!

100

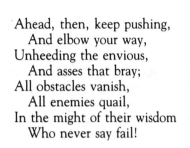

Ahead, then, keep pushing,
  And elbow your way,
Unheeding the envious,
  And asses that bray;
All obstacles vanish,
  All enemies quail,
In the might of their wisdom
  Who never say fail!

In life's early morning,
  In manhood's firm pride,
Let this be your motto
  Your footsteps to guide;
In storm and in sunshine,
  Whatever assail,
We'll onward and conquer,
  And never say fail!

LINCOLN'S RULES FOR LIVING

Do not worry, eat three square meals a day, say your prayers, be courteous to your creditors, keep your digestion good, steer clear of biliousness, exercise, go slow and go easy. May be there are other things that your special case requires to make you happy, but, my friend, these I reckon will give you a good lift.

Abraham Lincoln

I RESOLVE

To keep my health;
To do my work;
To live;
To see to it I grow and gain and give;
Never to look behind me for an hour;
To wait in meekness, and to walk in power;
But always fronting onward to the light,
Always and always facing toward the right.
Robbed, starved, defeated, fallen, wide-astray—
On, with what strength I have;
Back to the way.

102

IN A FRIENDLY SORT O' WAY

When a man ain't got a cent, and he's feeling kind
    o' blue,
An' the clouds hang dark an' heavy, an' won't let
    the sunshine through,
It's a great thing, O my brethren, for a feller just
    to lay
His hand upon your shoulder in a friendly sort o'
    way!
It makes a man feel curious, it makes the teardrop
    start,
An' you sort o' feel a flutter in the region of the
    heart:
You can look up and meet his eyes; you don't know
    what to say
When his hand is on your shoulder in a friendly
    sort o' way.

Oh, the world's a curious compound, with its honey
    and its gall,
With its cares and bitter crosses, but a good world,
    after all.
An' a good God must have made it—leastways,
    that is what I say,
When a hand is on my shoulder in a friendly sort
    o' way.

James Whitcomb Riley

103

NOBILITY

True worth is in being, not seeming;
　In doing each day that goes by,
Some little good—not in dreaming
　Of great things to do by and by.
For whatever men say in their blindness.
　And spite of the fancies of youth,
There's nothing so kingly as kindness,
　And nothing so royal as truth.

We get back our mete as we measure:
　We cannot do wrong and feel right;
Nor can we give pain and gain pleasure,
　For justice avenges each slight.
The air for the wing of the sparrow,
　The bush for the robin and wren,
But always the path that is narrow
　And straight for the children of men.

We cannot make bargains for blisses,
　Nor catch them like fishes in nets,
And sometimes the thing our life misses
　Helps more than the thing which it gets.
For good lieth not in pursuing,
　Nor gaining of great nor of small;
But just in the doing—and doing
　As we would be done by, is all.

Through envy, through malice, through hating
  Against the world early and late,
No jot of our courage abating,
  Our part is to work and to wait.
And slight is the sting of his trouble
  Whose winnings are less than his worth;
For he who is honest is noble,
  Whatever his fortunes or birth.

Alice Cary

JUNE

And what is so rare as a day in June?
  Then, if ever, come perfect days;
Then heaven tries the earth if it be in tune,
  And over it softly her warm ear lays;
Whether we look, or whether we listen,
We hear life murmur, or see it glisten;
Every clod feels a stir of might.
  An instinct within it that reaches and towers,
And, groping blindly above it for light,
  Climbs to a soul in grasses and flowers;
The flush of life may well be seen
  Thrilling back over hills and valleys;
The cowslip startles in meadows green,
  The buttercup catches the sun in its chalice,
And there's never a leaf nor a blade too mean
  To be some happy creature's palace;
The little bird sits at his door in the sun,
  Atilt like a blossom among the leaves,
And lets his illumined being o'errun
  With the deluge of summer it receives;
His mate feels the eggs beneath her wings,
And the heart in her dumb breast flutters and sings;
He sings to the wide world, and she to her nest—
In the nice ear of nature, which song is the best?

James Russell Lowell

SEND THEM TO BED WITH A KISS

O mothers, so weary, discouraged,
  Worn out with the cares of the day,
You often grow cross and impatient,
  Complain of the noise and the play;
For the day brings so many vexations,
  So many things going amiss;
But, mothers, whatever may vex you,
  Send the children to bed with a kiss!

The dear little feet wander often,
  Perhaps, from the pathway of right,
The dear little hands find new mischief
  To try you from morning till night;
But think of the desolate mothers
  Who'd give all the world for your bliss,
And, as thanks for your infinite blessings,
  Send the children to bed with a kiss!

For some day their noise will not vex you,
  The silence will hurt you far more;
You will long for their sweet childish voices,
  For a sweet childish face at the door;
And to press a child's face to your bosom,
  You'd give all the world for just this!
For the comfort 'twill bring you in sorrow,
  Send the children to bed with a kiss!

BEGIN AGAIN

Every day is a fresh beginning,
  Every morn is the world made new;
You who are weary of sorrow and sinning,
  Here is a beautiful hope for you—
  A hope for me and a hope for you.

All the past things are past and over,
  The tasks are done and the tears are shed;
Yesterday's errors let yesterday cover;
  Yesterday's wounds, which smarted and bled,
  Are healed with the healing which night has shed.

Yesterday now is a part of forever,
  Bound up in a sheaf, which God holds tight;
With glad days and sad days and bad days which
    never
    Shall visit us more with their bloom and their
      blight,
    Their fullness of sunshine or sorrowful night.

Let them go, since we cannot relive them,
  Cannot undo, and cannot atone;
God in His mercy, receive, forgive them;
  Only the new days are our own,
  Today is ours, and today alone.

Here are the skies all burnished brightly,
  Here is the spent Earth all reborn,
Here are the tired limbs springing lightly
  To face the sun and to share with the morn,
  In the chrism of dew and the cool of dawn.

Every day is a fresh beginning;
  Listen, my soul, to the glad refrain,
And, spite of old sorrow and older sinning,
  And puzzles forecasted and possible pain,
  Take heart with the day, and begin again.

IF WE KNEW

If we knew the cares and crosses
  Crowding round our neighbor's way;
If we knew the little losses,
  Sorely grievous day by day,
Would we then so often chide him
  For the lack of thrift and gain—
Casting o'er his life a shadow,
  Leaving on his heart a stain.

If we knew the silent story
  Quivering through the heart of pain,
Would our womanhood dare doom them
  Back to haunts of guilt again?
Life hath many a tangled crossing,
  Joy hath many a break of woe,
And the cheeks tear-washed seem whitest,
  This the blessed angels know.

Let us reach into our bosoms
  For the key to other lives,
And with love to erring nature,
  Cherish good that still survives;
So that when our disrobed spirits
  Soar to realms of light again,
We may say, dear Father, judge us
  As we judged our fellowmen.

PER PACEM AD LUCEM

I do not ask, O Lord, that life should always be
      A pleasant road;
I do not ask that Thou shouldst take from me
      Aught of its load.
I do not ask that flowers should always spring
      Beneath my feet—
Too well I know the poison and the sting
      Of things too sweet.

For one thing only, Lord, dear Lord, I plead—
      Lead me aright,
Though strength should falter and though heart
  should bleed—
      Through peace to light.

I do not ask my cross to understand,
      My way to see;
Better in darkness just to feel Thy hand
      And follow Thee.

I do not ask that Thou shouldst always shed
      Full radiance here;
Give but a ray of peace that I may walk
      Without a fear.

Joy is like restless day, but Peace divine
      Like quiet night.
Lead me, O Lord, till perfect day shall shine
      Through Peace to Light.

WHAT I LIVE FOR

I live for those who love me,
   Whose hearts are kind and true,
For the heaven that smiles above me,
   And awaits my spirit, too;
For the human ties that bind me,
For the task by God assigned me,
For the bright hopes left behind me,
   And the good that I can do.

I live to learn their story
   Who've suffered for my sake,
To emulate their glory,
   And to follow in their wake;
Bards, patriots, martyrs, sages,
The noble of all ages,
Whose deeds crowd history's pages
   And Time's great volume make.

I live to hold communion
   With all that is divine,
To feel there is a union
   'Twixt Nature's heart and mine;
To profit by affliction,
Reap truths from fields of fiction,
Grow wiser from conviction,
   And fulfill each grand design.

I live to hail that season,
  By gifted minds foretold,
When men shall rule by reason,
  And not alone by gold;
When man to man united,
And every wrong thing righted,
The whole world shall be lighted
  As Eden was of old.

I live for those who love me,
  For those who know me true,
For the Heaven that smiles above me,
  And awaits my spirit, too;
For the cause that lacks assistance,
For the wrong that needs resistance,
For the future in the distance,
  And the good that I can do.

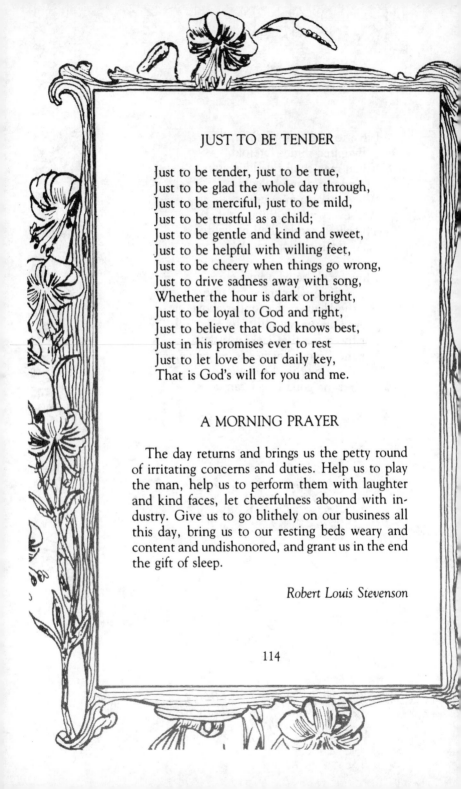

JUST TO BE TENDER

Just to be tender, just to be true,
Just to be glad the whole day through,
Just to be merciful, just to be mild,
Just to be trustful as a child;
Just to be gentle and kind and sweet,
Just to be helpful with willing feet,
Just to be cheery when things go wrong,
Just to drive sadness away with song,
Whether the hour is dark or bright,
Just to be loyal to God and right,
Just to believe that God knows best,
Just in his promises ever to rest
Just to let love be our daily key,
That is God's will for you and me.

A MORNING PRAYER

The day returns and brings us the petty round
of irritating concerns and duties. Help us to play
the man, help us to perform them with laughter
and kind faces, let cheerfulness abound with industry. Give us to go blithely on our business all
this day, bring us to our resting beds weary and
content and undishonored, and grant us in the end
the gift of sleep.

Robert Louis Stevenson

114

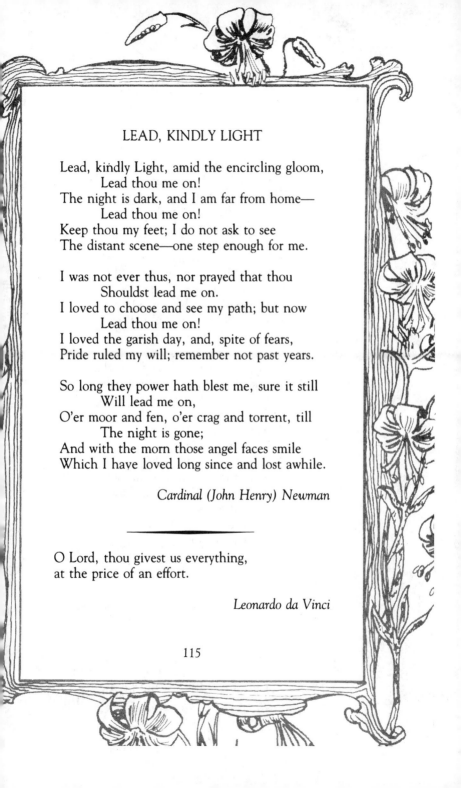

LEAD, KINDLY LIGHT

Lead, kindly Light, amid the encircling gloom,
    Lead thou me on!
The night is dark, and I am far from home—
    Lead thou me on!
Keep thou my feet; I do not ask to see
The distant scene—one step enough for me.

I was not ever thus, nor prayed that thou
    Shouldst lead me on.
I loved to choose and see my path; but now
    Lead thou me on!
I loved the garish day, and, spite of fears,
Pride ruled my will; remember not past years.

So long they power hath blest me, sure it still
    Will lead me on,
O'er moor and fen, o'er crag and torrent, till
    The night is gone;
And with the morn those angel faces smile
Which I have loved long since and lost awhile.

Cardinal (John Henry) Newman

O Lord, thou givest us everything,
at the price of an effort.

Leonardo da Vinci

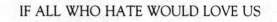

IF ALL WHO HATE WOULD LOVE US

If all who hate would love us,
   And all our loves were true,
The stars that swing above us
   Would brighten in the blue;
If cruel words were kisses,
   And every scowl a smile,
A better world than this is,
   Would hardly be worth while.
If purses would not tighten
   To meet a brother's need,
The load we bear would lighten
   Above the grave of greed.

If those who whine would whistle,
   And those who languish laugh,
The rose would rout the thistle,
   The grain outrun the chaff;
If hearts were only jolly,
   If grieving were forgot,
And tears of melancholy
   Were things that now are not;
Then love would kneel to duty,
   And all the world would seem
A bridal bower of beauty,
   A dream within a dream.

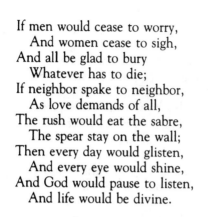

If men would cease to worry,
  And women cease to sigh,
And all be glad to bury
  Whatever has to die;
If neighbor spake to neighbor,
  As love demands of all,
The rush would eat the sabre,
  The spear stay on the wall;
Then every day would glisten,
  And every eye would shine,
And God would pause to listen,
  And life would be divine.

IF YOU HAVE A FRIEND WORTH LOVING

If you have a friend worth loving,
    Love him. Yes, and let him know
That you love him, ere life's evening
    Tinge his brow with sunset glow.
Why should good words ne'er be said
Of a friend—till he is dead?

If you hear a song that thrills you,
    Sung by any child of song,
Praise it. Do not let the singer
    Wait deservèd praises long.
Why should one who thrills your heart
Lack the joy you may impart?

If you hear a prayer that moves you
    By its humble, pleading tone,
Join it. Do not let the seeker
    Bow before his God alone.
Why should not your brother share
The strength of "two or three" in prayer?

If you see the hot tears falling
    From a brother's weeping eyes,
Share them. And by kindly sharing
    Own your kinship in the skies.
Why should anyone be glad
When a brother's heart is sad?

If a silvery laugh goes rippling
   Through the sunshine on his face,
Share it. 'Tis the wise man's saying—
   For both grief and joy a place.
There's health and goodness in the mirth
In which an honest laugh has birth.

If your work is made more easy
   By a friendly, helping hand,
Say so. Speak out brave and truly
   Ere the darkness veil the land.
Should a brother workman dear
Falter for a word of cheer?

Scatter thus your seeds of kindness
   All enriching as you go—
Leave them. Trust the Harvest-Giver;
   He will make each seed to grow.
So, until the happy end,
Your life shall never lack a friend.

SOMEBODY

Somebody did a golden deed;
Somebody proved a friend in need;
Somebody sang a beautiful song;
Somebody smiled the whole day long;
Somebody thought, " 'Tis sweet to live";
Somebody said, "I'm glad to give";
Somebody fought a valiant fight;
Somebody lived to shield the right;
    Was that "somebody" you?

A READER'S PRAYER

Lord, let me never slight the meaning nor the moral of anything I read. Make me respect my mind so much that I dare not read what has no meaning or moral. Help me choose with equal care my friends and my books, because they are both for life. Show me that as in a river, so in reading, the depths hold more of strength and beauty than the shallows. Teach me to value art without being blind to thought. Keep me from caring more for much reading than for careful reading; for books than the Book. Give me an ideal that will let me read only the best, and when that is done, stop me. Repay me with power to teach others, and then help me to say from a disciplined mind a grateful Amen.

OPPORTUNITY

Master of human destinies am I.
Fame, love, and fortune on my footsteps wait,
Cities and fields I walk; I penetrate
Deserts and seas remote, and, passing by
Hovel, and mart, and palace, soon or late
I knock unbidden once at every gate!
If sleeping, wake—if feasting, rise before

I turn away. It is the hour of fate,
And they who follow me reach every state
Mortals desire, and conquer every foe
Save death; but those who doubt or hesitate,
Condemned to failure, penury and woe,
Seek me in vain and uselessly implore,
I answer not, and I return no more.

TAKEN AT THE FLOOD

There is a tide in the affairs of men
Which, taken at the flood, leads on to fortune;
Omitted, all the voyage of their life
Is bound in shallows and in miseries.
On such a full sea are we now afloat,
And we must take the current when it serves,
Or lose our ventures.

Shakespeare

THE LORD'S PRAYER

After this manner therefore pray ye:

Our Father which art in heaven, hallowed be Thy name. Thy kingdom come. Thy will be done on earth as it is in heaven. Give us this day our daily bread. And forgive us our debts, as we forgive our debtors. And lead us not into temptation, but deliver us from evil; for Thine is the kingdom, and the power and the glory, forever. Amen.

Matthew 6: 9-13

GRATITUDE TO GOD

Notwithstanding all that I have suffered, notwithstanding all the pain and weariness and anxiety and sorrow that necessarily enter into life, and the inward errings that are worse than all, I would end my record with a devout thanksgiving to the great Author of my being. For more and more am I unwilling to make my gratitude to Him what is commonly called "a thanksgiving for mercies,"— for any benefits or blessings that are peculiar to myself, or my friends, or indeed to any man. Instead of this, I would have it to be gratitude for all that belongs to my life and being—for joy and sorrow, for health and sickness, for success and disappointment, for virtue and for temptation, for life and death; because I believe that all is meant for good.

THE INEVITABLE

I like the man who faces what he must
    With step triumphant and a heart of cheer;
    Who fights the daily battle without fear;
Sees his hopes fail, yet keeps unfaltering trust
That God is God; that somehow, true and just
    His plans work out for mortals; not a tear
    Is shed when fortune, which the world holds
       dear,
Falls from his grasp; better, with love, a crust
Than living in dishonor; envies not,
    Nor loses faith in man; but does his best
Nor ever mourns over his humbler lot,
    But with a smile and words of hope, gives zest
To every toiler; he alone is great,
Who by a life heroic conquers fate.

SUCCESS

That man is a success who has lived well, laughed
often and loved much; who has gained the respect
of intelligent men and the love of children; who
has filled his niche and accomplished his task; who
leaves the world better than he found it, whether
by an improved poppy, a perfect poem or a rescued
soul; who never lacked appreciation of earth's beauty
or failed to express it; who looked for the best in
others and gave the best he had.

Robert Louis Stevenson

MY MOTHERS BIBLE

This book is all that's left me now,
    Tears will unbidden start,—
With faltering lip and throbbing brow
    I press it to my heart.
For many generations past,
    Here is our family tree:
My mother's hand this Bible clasped;
    She, dying, gave it me.

Ah! well do I remember those
    Whose names these records bear,
Who round the hearthstone used to close
    After the evening prayer
And speak of what these pages said,
    In tones my heart would thrill!
Though they are with the silent dead,
    Here are they living still!

My father read this holy book
    To brothers, sister, dear;
How calm was my poor mother's look,
    Who leaned God's word to hear.
Her angel face—I see it yet!
    What thronging memories come!
Again that little group is met
    Within the halls of home!

Thou truest friend man ever knew,
　Thy constancy I've tried;
Where all were false I found thee true,
　My counsellor and guide.
The mines of earth no treasure give
　That could this volume buy:
In teaching me the way to live,
　It taught me how to die.

125

LIFE

(A Literary Curiosity.)

Why all this toil for triumphs of an hour?

Young

Life's a short summer—man is but a flower.

Dr. Johnson

By turns we catch the fatal breath and die;

Pope

The cradle and the tomb, alas! so nigh.

Prior

To be is better far than not to be,

Sewell

Though all man's life may seem a tragedy;

Spenser

But light cares speak when mighty griefs are dumb

Daniel

The bottom is but shallow whence they come.

Sir Walter Raleigh

Thy fate is the common fate of all;

Longfellow

Unmingled joys can here no man befall;

Southwell

Nature to each allots his proper sphere,

Congreve

Fortune makes folly her peculiar care.

Churchill

Custom does often reason overrule,

Rochester

And throw a cruel sunshine on a fool.

Armstrong

Live well; how long or short permit to Heaven.

Milton

They who forgive most shall be most forgiven.

Bailey

Sin may be clasped so close we cannot see its face

French

Vile intercourse where virtue has no place.

Somerville

Then keep each passion down, however dear,

Thompson

Thou pendulum betwixt a smile and tear.

Byron

Her sensual snares let faithless pleasure lay,

Smollett

With craft and skill to ruin and betray.

Crabbe

Soar not too high to fall, but stoop to rise;

Massinger

We masters grow of all that we despise.

Crowley

Oh, then, renounce that impious self-esteem,

Beattie

Riches have wings and grandeur is a dream.

Cowper

Think not ambition wise because 'tis brave.

Sir Wm. Davenant

The paths of glory lead but to the grave.

Gray

127

What is ambition? 'Tis a glorious cheat,
Willis

Only destructive to the brave and great.
Addison

What's all the gaudy glitter of a crown?
Dryden

The way to bliss lies not on beds of down.
Francis Quarles

How long we live, not years, but actions tell;
Watkins

That man lives twice who lives the first life well.
Herrick

Make, then, while yet ye may, your God your friend,
William Mason

Whom Christians worship, yet not comprehend.
Hill

The trust that's given, guard, and to yourself be just;
Dano

For live we how we may, yet die we must.
Shakespeare